You've Got To

STAND

for
Something!

Understanding & Restoring America's
Founding Principles

ANDREW FOY, MD

NIMBLE BOOKS LLC

Nimble Books LLC

1521 Martha Avenue

Ann Arbor, MI, USA 48103

http://www.NimbleBooks.com

wfz@nimblebooks.com

+1.734-330-2593

Version 1.0; last saved 2010-09-14.

Printed in the United States of America

ISBN-13: 978-1-60888-019-5

The paper used in this publication meets the minimum requiremen
of the American National Standard for Information Sciences
Permanence of Paper for Printed Library Materials, ANSI Z39.4
1992. The paper is acid-free and lignin-free.

Epigraph

"The spirit of 1776 is not dead. It has only been slumbering. The body of the American people is substantially republican. But their virtuous feelings have been played on by some fact with more fiction; they have been the dupes of artful maneuvers and made for a moment to be willing instruments in forging chains for themselves. But time and truth have dissipated the delusion and opened their eyes."

—Thomas Jefferson, 1799

iv

CONTENTS (INCLUDING FIGURES)

YOU'VE GOT TO STAND FOR SOMETHING

Just as the founding fathers pledged their "lives, fortunes and sacred honor" to the cause of freedom when they signed The Declaration of Independence; now is the time to stand up for the foundational principles of America; for yourself, for your family, and for your country.

> "You've got to stand for something or you'll fall for anything."

> —*Aaron Tippin*

PRINCIPLES OF THE AMERICAN REVOLUTION

> "We hold these truths to be self-evident, that all men are created equal, that they are endowed by their Creator with certain unalienable Rights, that among these are Life, Liberty and the pursuit of Happiness.—That to secure these rights, Governments are instituted among Men, deriving their just powers from the consent of the governed."

> *—The Declaration of Independence July 4, 1776*

The rights to **life, liberty and the pursuit of happiness,** along with **property rights,** which the Founders regarded as fundamental, are known as natural rights or liberty rights. They protect the rights of each individual to **freedom and autonomy;** to take all the actions required to support the furtherance, fulfillment and enjoyment of one's *own* life. These rights are rooted in the philosophical teachings of natural rights theorists. Critical in the thinking leading to the American Revolution were the efforts of John Locke, who sought to determine man's "universal rights" or "objective rights", meaning the rights bestowed on man as a result being man. According to Locke and his contemporaries, who most notably include the Founding Fathers—if man has certain rights based merely on his existence then the proper role of government is to protect those **natural nights, rather than** to be the dispenser of **an arbitrarily defined bundle of rights.**

In Locke's *Second Treatise of Government* he writes,

> "To understand political power right, and derive it from its original, we must consider what state all men are naturally in, and this is, a state of perfect freedom to order their actions, and dispose of their possessions, and persons as they think fit, within the bounds of the law of nature, without asking leave, or depending upon the will of any

other man ... But though this be a state of liberty, yet it is not a state of license ... The state of nature has a law of nature to govern it ... and reason, which is that law, teaches all mankind, that being all equal and independent, no one ought to harm another in his life, health, liberty, or possessions."[1]

According to Locke, the **desire for happiness and the pursuit of happiness** have the character of an absolute or natural right. He wrote, "Nature ... has put into man a desire of happiness, and an aversion to misery" and "men ... must be allowed to pursue their happiness, nay, cannot be hindered."[1] **Liberty** is the social condition which frees men from these hindrances and therefore, man has an absolute right to individual freedom or liberty.

In the *Constitution of Liberty*, F.A. Hayek wrote,

> "[Liberty] describes the absence of a particular obstacle—coercion by other men [or government] ... It does not assure us of any particular opportunities, but leaves it to us to decide what use we shall make of the circumstances in which we find ourselves." [2]

Therefore, liberty is inextricably bound with personal responsibility and self-reliance. Liberty means that the individual has both the opportunity and the burden of choice and that he must bear the consequences of his actions. **A free society cannot function or maintain itself unless its members firmly believe that each individual should occupy the position that results from his actions.**

Further, since happiness and liberty presuppose life, man must have an absolute right to his **life**, which also means he has the right to preserve it. And while nature has put into man the strong desire for

---

[1] Locke, John. *Two Treatises of Government.* London & Vermont: Everyman, 1993.

[2] Hayek, F. A. *The Constitution of Liberty.* Chicago: The University of Chicago Press, 1960.

happiness and self-preservation, it is only man's capacity for reason (the law of nature) that teaches him what is necessary to attain happiness and preserve his own life, and it is reason which endows him with the capacity for self-government. Reason teaches that life cannot be preserved, let alone enjoyed, except in a state of peace where no individual has the right to infringe on the natural rights of another human being. Therefore, if man is to realize his natural rights to the fullest extent possible, he must live in a state of peace. The prominent 20th century philosopher Leo Strauss summarized Locke's natural law in the following words:

> "the law of nature is nothing other than the sum of the dictates of reason in regard to men's 'mutual security' or to 'the peace and safety' of mankind."[3]

The concepts of natural rights and natural law were at the core of the American Revolution. For this reason, the revolution of 1776 was not merely a revolution to gain independence from a distant power, but more importantly, it was a revolution to gain individual liberty—freedom of man from government-over-man. This freedom was not to be given occasionally or arbitrarily by favor of King or Parliament but was to be assured governmentally in accordance with the law of nature. The unprecedented principles exhibited in The Declaration of Independence, **"that all men are created equal, that they are endowed by their Creator with certain unalienable Rights, that among these are Life, Liberty and the pursuit of Happiness"**, was one of the greatest acts of Man's spirit and mind in all history. Reflecting on these unprecedented principles in a letter to John

---

[3] Strauss, Leo. *Natural Right and History.* Chicago: The University of Chicago Press, 1953.

Adams, Thomas Jefferson wrote, **"If ever the morals of a people could be made the basis of their own government, it is our case."**[4]

Lord Acton, the influential English historian and classical liberal theorist, captured the spirit of the American Revolution when he wrote,

> "Europe seemed incapable of becoming the home of free States. It was from America that the plain ideas that men ought to mind their own business, and that the nation is responsible to Heaven for the acts of state—ideas long locked in the breasts of solitary thinkers, and hidden among Latin folios—burst forth like a conqueror upon the world they were destined to transform, under the title of the Rights of Man."[5]

---

[4] The Library of America. *Jefferson*. New York: Library Classics of the United States of America, 1984.

[5] Acton, John. *The History of Freedom and Other Essays*. New York: Cosimo Classics, 2005.

Principles of American Government

> "Liberty and good government do not exclude each other. And there are excellent reasons why they should go together. Liberty is not a means to a higher political end. It is itself the highest political end." —Lord Acton, 1877

> "WE THE PEOPLE of the United States, in order to form a more perfect Union, establish Justice, insure domestic Tranquility, provide for the common Defense, promote the general Welfare, and secure the Blessings of Liberty to ourselves and our posterity, do ordain and establish this CONSTITUTION for the United States of America."

> *—The Constitution of the United States*

This passage from the Constitution underscores the founding principles of American Government, which are in perfect concordance with Locke's law of nature or Strauss's "sum of the dictates of reason" required for securing "the peace and safety." For Locke, the proper role of government is to ensure "that all men may be restrained from invading others' rights, and from doing hurt to one another."

We can restate the basic role of American government then as: to secure peace, which is the condition ultimately required for man to realize his natural rights to the fullest extent. For the founders, the most important question that arose in the wake of the revolution became: **How to form a government capable of securing peace and thus capable of protecting the natural rights of the individual but incapable of usurping these rights?** Regarding this question, many Americans today wrongly believe the founders' answer was to create a democratic government. However, the founders rightly understood that pure democracy was utterly incapable of protecting the rights of the individual, so instead, they established a republican form of Government. In a republic, power is delegated from the citizens to their elected representatives and exercised under a system of laws. To this day, "We pledge allegiance to the Flag of the United States of America and to the Republic for which it stands."

In *The Federalist No. 39* James Madison wrote,

> "The first question that offers itself is, whether the general form and aspect of the government be strictly republican? It is evident that no other form would be reconcilable with the genius of the people of America; with the fundamental principles of the revolution; or with the honorable determination, which animates every votary of freedom, to rest all our political experiments on the capacity of mankind for self-government."[6]

Understanding the difference between a republic and a democracy is a critical concept if one is to truly understand the principles of American government. **Unlike the republican form of government, democracy is not a sufficient condition to secure individual liberty because it necessarily subjects the individual to the binding will of the majority.** From this perspective, we can say that democracy is the majority unlimited, or rule by omnipotent majority without regard to the rights of the individual or minority.

This point was articulated by Madison in *The Federalist No. 10*:

> "A common passion or interest will, in almost every case be felt by a majority of the whole; a communication and concert results from the form of Government [Democracy] itself; and there is nothing to check the inducements to sacrifice the weaker party, or an obnoxious individual. Hence it is, that such Democracies have ever been spectacles of turbulence and contention; have ever been found incompatible with personal security, or the rights of

---

[6] Madison, James. The Federalist No. *39*. *The Federalist Papers.* New York: Bantam Books, 1982.

property; and have in general been as short in their lives, as they have been violent in their deaths." [7]

Echoing Madison's sentiment, John Adams wrote in a letter to Thomas Jefferson, "Democracy never lasts long, it soon wastes, exhausts and murders itself. There has never been a democracy yet that did not commit suicide." [8]

Individual liberty is an impossible end if man is to be subject to the will of the majority because the majority is nothing but a group of individuals and within this group of individuals many opinions exist, which makes it impossible to express a unifying opinion. The will of the majority is not much more than the will of those individuals governing the majority. Ultimately what exists, in the words of American journalist and political theorist Rose Wilder Lane, "is a man, or a few men, in power over many men." [9] Under this condition, individual liberty and self-government cannot survive because it is impossible for a man or a few men to represent "the multitude of diverse human beings with an infinite variety of purposes and desires and fluctuating wills." [10]

At the time of the American Revolution, the people of Great Britain had discarded the century's older idea and system of the divine right of kings and replaced it with the unlimited power of Parliament, the national legislature; representing the absolute power of the majority and continuing the tradition of government-over-man. This reflected the English tradition of Government having a supreme authority over man in an environment that was rigidly stratified into distinct classes. The British "Constitution," according to Madison, was nothing but the aggregate of all laws, which Parliament could

---

[7] Madison, James. The Federalist No. 10. *The Federalist Papers*. New York: Bantam Books, 1982.

[8] McCullough, David. *John Adams*. New York: Simon & Schuster, 2001.

[9] Lane, R. W. *Give Me Liberty*. New York: Longmans, Green And Co., 1936.

[10] *Ibid.*

make or change at will. In *The Federalist No. 53* he wrote, "Even in Great-Britain, where the principles of political and civil liberty have been most discussed; and where we hear most of the rights of the constitution, it is maintained that **the authority of the parliament is transcendent and uncontrollable.**"[11]

As the founders understood, a republic offers the only solution for protecting individuals, with their diverse array of interests and fluctuating wills, against the uncontrollable power of government. This is achieved by limiting the government's power, and binding it to a written constitution, which is adopted by the people and changeable only by the people through the amendment process. Therefore, a republic is a constitutionally limited government of the representative type at the federal and state level with its limited powers divided between three separate branches (executive, legislative and judicial). The founders understood that establishing a republican form of government was absolutely necessary for securing the aims of the American revolution, namely, to gain and maintain individual freedom or freedom of man from government-over-man.

Limited government is a necessary condition for self-government. The limited powers of the United States government are clearly enumerated in the Constitution. In this way, the limited quantity of its powers predictably limits the government's potential threat to the liberties of all people. Further, these constitutional powers set the limits of the duties that people can assign to a system of government. Without these limits, there would be no restraints in effect to prevent government from sacrificing the rights of individuals of a weaker party. These duties cannot be changed at the will of government or by the whims of majority or a "claimed majority." This aspect of

---

[11] Madison, James. The Federalist No. 53. *The Federalist Papers.* New York: Bantam Books, 1982.

republican government is necessary for maintaining individual liberty. According to Friedrich Hayek, Nobel Prize winning economist and one of the most influential political philosophers of the 20th century:

> "A free society certainly needs permanent means of restricting the powers of government, no matter what the particular objective of the moment may be. And the Constitution which the new American nation was to give itself was definitely meant not merely as a regulation of the derivation of power but as a constitution of liberty, a constitution that would protect the individual against all arbitrary coercion."

In *The Federalist No.* 41 Madison reviews the limited powers conferred on the government of the new union:

> " ... they may be reduced into different classes as they relate to the following different objects;—1. security against foreign danger—2. regulation of the intercourse with foreign nations—3. maintenance of harmony and proper intercourse among the States—4. certain miscellaneous objects of general utility—5. restraint of the States from certain injurious acts—6. provisions for giving due efficacy to all these powers."[12]

Thomas Jefferson reaffirmed the necessity for limited government in his First Inaugural Address as President when he stated:

> " ... What more is necessary to make us happy and a prosperous people? Still one thing more, fellow-citizens—a wise and frugal Government, which shall restrain men from injuring one another, shall leave them otherwise free to regulate their own pursuits of industry and improvement, and shall not take from the mouth of labor the bread it has earned. This is the sum of good government."[13]

---

[12] Madison, James. The Federalist No. 41. *The Federalist Papers.* New York: Bantam Books, 1982.

[13] Jefferson, *supra.*

"It will not be denied that power is of an encroaching nature, and that it ought to be effectually restrained from passing the limits assigned to it."

—James Madison, 1788

"The natural progress of things is for liberty to yield and government to gain ground."

—Thomas Jefferson, 1788

The Principle of Providing for the "General Welfare"

No concept in our founding documents has been more misconstrued than the concept of the government's role in providing for the "public good" or "general welfare." It shouldn't be surprising then that the vast majority of problematic extensions of governmental power occur under the banner of "providing for the public good." Under those auspices government has become involved in providing cradle-to-grave education, health care and economic security; funding for housing, automobiles and cell phones; bailing out banks, auto companies and any other businesses deemed appropriate; and funding for corporations in areas such as energy production, health care and construction. All of this places a tremendous burden on the individual for he must involuntarily turn over an increasing amount of power and personal possessions to government for projects which have no immediate bearing on him or his family and which may come at the expense of pursuing his own interests.

To formulate an independent view as to which projects qualify as "public goods," one must consider the original intent of the phrase. American government is rooted in Locke's natural law teaching, which is that government is responsible to provide the sum of laws necessary for the conservation and defense of man against other men. Therefore, the government's role in providing for the public good is nothing more (or less) than the sum of public services required to secure peace or to protect men from other men. Despite the simplicity of this foundational principle, it is routinely violated by public officials in the name of providing for the general welfare.

It is important to note that the authority granted to Congress in the Constitution "to provide for the common defense and general welfare of the United States," was hotly contested from the onset, which led Madison to explain the purpose and intentions of the clause in *Federalist No. 41*. He wrote,

> "Some who have not denied the necessity of the power of taxation, have grounded a very fierce attack against the Constitution on the language in which it is defined. It has been urged and echoed, that the power 'to lay and collect taxes, duties, imposts and excises, to pay the debts and provide for the common defense and general welfare of the United States,' amounts to an unlimited commission to exercise every power which may be alleged to be necessary for the common defense or general welfare. No stronger proof could be given of the distress under which these writers labor for objections, than their stooping to such a misconstruction ... what color can the objection have, when a specification of the objects alluded to by these general terms, immediately follows; and is not even separated by a longer pause than a semicolon."[14]

To find exactly what Madison is referring to, that **"is not even separated by a longer pause than a semicolon"** we would direct readers to review Article 1, Section 8 of The Constitution. A brief review of the specified objects includes:

> To borrow money on the credit of the United States.

---

[14] Madison, James. The Federalist No. 41. *The Federalist Papers*. New York: Bantam Books, 1982.

To regulate commerce with foreign nations, and among the several states, and with the Indian tribes.

To establish a uniform rule of naturalization, and uniform laws on the subjects of bankruptcies throughout the Unites States.

To coin money.

To promote the progress of science and useful arts by securing for a limited time patents to authors and inventors.

To constitute tribunals.

To define and punish felonies committed on the oceans.

To declare war

To raise and support the army and navy.

To make all laws necessary for carrying into execution the specified powers.

If the commerce clause is interpreted as Madison and the founders originally intended and not as an "unlimited commission for the federal government to exercise power" than the government's Constitutional duty to provide for the "general welfare" is nothing more than the sum of governmental duties necessary to maintain peace and prevent men from injuring one another.

> "A government big enough to give you everything you want is a government big enough to take from you everything you have."
>
> —*Gerald Ford,* 1974

Separation of Church and State

> "Congress shall make no law respecting an establishment of religion, or prohibiting the free exercise thereof."
>
> —*Amendment* 1, *The Constitution of the United States*

Separation of church and state is critical to natural law philosophy. According to Locke, if there is to be a law knowable by the light of nature it must consist of a set of rules whose validity is based on reason and does not presuppose any particular religious belief. Natural law is therefore the law of reason and America is a country founded on reason and a belief in the power of man's mind. Natural law is the sum of all dictates necessary to secure peace; it is not the law of religion. The Founding fathers understood that the mixture of government and religion could impose violations on the natural rights of the individual.

In a letter to the General Assembly of the Commonwealth of Virginia, Madison wrote,

> "What influence in fact have ecclesiastical establishments had on Civil Society? In some instances they have been seen to erect a spiritual tyranny on the ruins of the Civil authority; in many instances they have been seen upholding the thrones of political tyranny; in no instance have they been seen the guardians of the liberties of the people. Rulers who wished to subvert the public liberty, may have found an established Clergy convenient auxiliaries. A just Government instituted to secure and perpetuate it needs them not. Such a Government will be best supported by protecting every Citizen in the enjoyment of his Religion with the same equal hand which protects his person and his property; by neither invading the equal rights of any Sect, nor suffering any Sect to invade those of another ... The Religion then of every man must be left to the conviction and conscience of every man; and it is the right of every man to exercise it as these may dictate. This right is in its nature an unalienable right."[15]

---

[15] The Library of America. *Madison*. New York: Library Classics of the United States of America, 1999.

Charity and Service in a Free Society

In a free society, charity and service are individual and personal undertakings and, as a rule, cannot be subject to coercion if liberty is to be maintained. In his authoritative work on freedom, *The Constitution of Liberty*, F.A. Hayek explained the role of charity and service in a free society,

> "By common opinion our chief concern is the welfare of our family. But we also show our appreciation and approval of others by making them our friends and their aims ours. To choose our associates and generally those whose needs we make our concern is an essential part of freedom and of the moral conceptions of a free society ... It is one of the fundamental rights and duties of a free man to decide what and whose needs appear to him most important."[16]

However, if politicians have the power to redistribute wealth for the purpose of meeting the needs of society, by definition, the individual is constrained from the fully autonomous exercise of his right, and responsibility, for charity and service. Therefore, the Constitution made no provisions for the government to be involved in providing charity or redistributing wealth in the interest of protecting individual freedom against mob rule and tyranny.

Still there are many people in a society who for many reasons do not have the means to provide certain necessities for themselves. This ultimately leads to the question, **"What of the poor?"** Based on America's founding principles the answer is, **"you will not be stopped from helping them"** and therein lies the essence of charity and personal responsibility in a free society. As Hayek pointed out, it is the responsibility of free individuals to decide for who they would like

---

[16] Hayek, F. A. *The Constitution of Liberty*. Chicago: The University of Chicago Press, 1960.

to be charitable and in what way they would like to provide service. There is no textbook known that can offer an individual the insights that voluntary service can provide. These opportunities to connect with other human beings show us that we are more alike than different, that we can provide the services that others need, and that we can be the recipients of much more than we offered. It offers a framework for trust-building and the much-needed sense of gratification for both provider and beneficiary that become the building blocks for a successful relationship that is mutually advantageous. In sum, it offers the ultimate expression of individual freedom.

Today, unfortunately, we have literally hundreds of government programs dedicated to providing for peoples' needs, and while these programs rely on unwarranted extensions of the Constitutional provision for the "general welfare", it would be unfair to their recipients to end them abruptly. However, a more historically and philosophically sound understanding of the government's proper Constitutional role should serve as the basis for stopping the creation of new programs and unwinding existing programs.

Grover Cleveland took a very principled stand on government redistribution in 1887 when a sizeable portion of Texas had suffered from a severe drought. Congress had authorized seeds to be granted to the farmers there to stave hunger, but President Cleveland, a Democrat in an era still struggling with Reconstruction after the American Civil War, vetoed the bill, even though it provided for the relief of formerly Confederate Texas. In a letter to the house on February 16th, 1887 he wrote,

> "And yet I feel obliged to withhold my approval of the plan as proposed by this bill, to indulge a benevolent and charitable sentiment through the appropriation of public funds for that purpose. I can find no warrant for such an appropriation in the Constitution, and I do not believe that

the power and duty of the general government ought to be extended to the relief of individual suffering which is in no manner properly related to the public service or benefit. The friendliness and charity of our countrymen can always be relied upon to relieve their fellow-citizens in misfortune. This has been repeatedly and quite lately demonstrated. Federal aid in such cases encourages the expectation of paternal care on the part of the government and weakens the sturdiness of our national character, while it prevents the indulgence among our people of that kindly sentiment and conduct which strengthen the bonds of a common brotherhood."[17]

Cleveland clearly understood the principles of the American revolution and of American government. These are the principles of **individual freedom, personal responsibility and limited government**. It is these principles in which true patriotism, color-blind to party affiliation, is firmly rooted.

> "A society that does not recognize that each individual has values of his own which he is entitled to follow can have no respect for the dignity of the individual and cannot really know freedom."
>
> *—F.A. Hayek*

Equality Under The Law

> "Jus cuique, the golden rule, is all the equality that can be supported or defended by reason or common sense."
>
> *—John Adams,* 1787

Another idea, often misrepresented, about America's founding principles is that all individuals have a right to "equality of

---

[17] Parker, GF. The Writings and Speeches of Grover Cleveland. Cassell Publishing, 1892.

conditions" or at least to "equality of opportunity." The Declaration begins, "We hold these truths to be self evident, that all men are created equal, that they are endowed by their creator with certain unalienable rights..." What this means is that all individuals have the right to be treated equally under the law.

Unfortunately, upon America's founding, equality under the law was not granted to all individuals. However, as the country evolved, this situation was corrected in a manner consistent with our core principles. Thanks to the genius of our Framers, who separated power among three branches of government, our courts have been able to take the lead by standing up to enforce equal protection, as demanded by the Constitution even when the executive and legislative branches, and often the public as well, were unwilling to confront wrongful discrimination.

However, as our country has evolved, the legislative branch has moved to pass legislation whose intent is to discriminate - this is most apparent in the area of tax policy where citizens are taxed at different rates depending on their earnings and certain businesses are given targeted tax exemptions and subsidies usually as a result of the strength of their lobbying interest.

Furthermore, much discriminatory legislation has been passed in the name of bringing about equality of conditions or equality of opportunity, which are antithetical to the aims of free society. That is why it is so important to appreciate the uniquely American principle of equality under the law. No other equality is possible in a free society. Because individuals are not equal in terms of their skill, industry or birth, the only way to equalize conditions would be through means of arbitrary force or coercion.

In *The Federalist No.* 10 Madison supports the natural law position, expressed by John Locke in his *Two Treatises of Government* that in a free society the rights of property originate from the diversity in the faculties of men.

> "The protection of these faculties is the first object of government. From the protection of different and unequal faculties of acquiring property, the possession of different degrees and kinds of property immediately results."[18]

At the time of the American Revolution and the framing of the US Constitution, French philosophers were challenging Locke's interpretation of natural law and the protection of private property. They were advocating for legislation that would force conditions of equality and bring about a perfect egalitarian society. From their beginning, these ideas were recognized as toxic, immoral, and were strongly rebuked by our founders who most notably included John Adams who summarized his position in a letter to John Taylor. (It must be mentioned that multiple founders including Jefferson and Paine endorsed the French Revolution in response to the aristocratic structure of French society, but they never endorsed the principles that drove the revolution.)

> "That all men are born to equal rights is clear. Every being has a right to his own, as moral, as sacred, as any other has. This is as indubitable as a moral government in the universe. But to teach that all men are born with equal powers and faculties, to equal influence in society, to equal property and advantages through life, is as gross a fraud, as glaring an imposition on the credulity of the people, as ever was practiced by monks, by Druids, by Brahmins, by priests of the immortal Lama, or by the self-styled philosophers of the French Revolution. For honor's sake, Mr. Taylor, for

---

[18] Madison, James. The Federalist No. 10. *The Federalist Papers*. New York: Bantam Books, 1982.

truth and virtue's sake, let American philosophers and politicians despise it."[19]

There can be nothing close to the attainment of "absolute equality" in a nation who believes that the protection of individual liberty is the ultimate end of government. In a free society, we are not rewarded for our mere existence or even for our talent but for using our talent correctly. Despite this fact, there are those who believe that individuals not only have the right to life, liberty, and the pursuit of happiness, but to that position in the social scale to which their talents entitle them. Individuals who hold this view often do not recognize that this concept is totally irreconcilable with the principles of free society. To claim that a man's talents entitle him to any particular position would necessarily mean that some agency has the right and power to place men in particular positions according to its judgment. This is not a condition of freedom but one of servitude. All that a free society has to offer is an opportunity of searching for a suitable position, with all the attendant risk and uncertainty which such a search for a market for one's gifts must involve.

On Social Engineering

"Human reason can neither predict nor deliberately shape its own future. Its advance consists in finding out where it has been wrong...Progress by its very nature cannot be planned."

—F.A. Hayek, 1948

The founding fathers were strong individualists. Properly understood, individualism wisely appreciates the limitations of individual knowledge and recognizes the fact that no person, small group or government can know all that is known among the mass of

[19] Kirk, Russell. *The Conservative Mind.* Washington, DC: Regnery Publishing, Inc. 1953.

individuals in society. Individualism postulates that an individual can only effectively apply reason to the situations and circumstances he has intimate knowledge of, his own affairs; and not those for which he cannot have sufficient knowledge of, the affairs of others.

Due to the limitations on man's knowledge and interests an individual cannot know more than a tiny part of the whole of society and therefore, all that can enter into his motives are the immediate effects which his actions, whether completely selfish or totally altruistic, will have on the sphere he knows. Individualists believe that problems, whether social or economic, are best solved by the voluntary and spontaneous action of individuals pursuing their own interests and NOT by the coercive action of the state. Therefore, the founders favored a government that was limited to protect individual freedom and self-government and avoid experiments in social engineering.

The founding fathers were students of history and as such, recognized the inherent folly in the belief that government is capable of solving society's problems. Government is nothing more than a group of individuals and as such cannot possibly take into account all the permutations, variability and fluctuating desires of the mass of individuals who compose society. For this reason, American government was not established to solve problems but rather to create conditions in which individuals could solve their own problems. The founders wisely recognized that much for which the coercive action of the state is invoked can be done better by the spontaneous and voluntary collaboration of individuals.

One of the most prominent individualists of the modern era was Friedrich Hayek. He was an Austrian economist, philosopher and intellectual considered to be one of the most important economists and political philosophers of the twentieth century. He shared the 1974 Nobel Prize in Economics for his pioneering work in the theory of money and economic fluctuations. His own life experiences, growing up in Europe during the time when socialism was gaining influence and power, convinced him of the misguided nature of social engineering, which refers to the government's efforts to influence social behaviors and economic outcomes on a large scale by means of coercion. He experienced the real life consequences of social engineering first hand.

Hayek's central thesis in his seminal work, *The Road to Serfdom*, is that through the inevitable mismanagement of resources and goods at the disposal of the state—all forms of collectivism and social engineering lead eventually to tyranny. Hayek used the Soviet Union and Nazi Germany as examples of countries that had progressed through the phases of collectivism and social engineering and reached the point of tyranny. Hayek argued that disagreement regarding the practical implementation of any economic plan combined with the inadequacy of the planners' resource management would necessitate coercion in order for anything to be achieved. According to Hayek, the failure of central planning would be perceived by some in the public as an absence of sufficient power by the state to implement an otherwise good idea. This would lead the public to vote more power to the state, assisting in the rise of a "strong man" perceived to be capable of getting the job done. Following these developments, a country would be driven into outright totalitarianism. For Hayek, this journey, inadvertently set upon by social engineering and central planning, ends in the destruction of all individual economic and personal freedoms.

The thesis of the modern day social engineer is that by using the force of government, mankind can be changed and molded to conform to a master plan. The modern day social engineer either knows nothing of nature's laws or chooses to ignore them. Instead, he has his man-made and variable laws of compulsions, prohibitions, and other restrictions on the free actions of individuals. By means of these laws, he claims he can compel the behavior of men in a manner that will benefit the good of mankind.

In a 1953 speech given by Admiral Ben Moreell, the chairman of Jones & Laughlin Steel Corp, to the Society of Automotive Engineers he said,

> "Social engineers use their raw material—human beings—to create products designed to serve and please their own fancy—and frequently to satisfy their craving for personal power. And often they do this by appealing to the baser traits of man—laziness, greed, selfishness and irresponsibility ... [they] also are given to extensive planning and experimenting. They construct models in order to secure a better idea of how they may control the full-scale project. But actually, experience has shown that almost always the ultimate effects are the opposite of those which they claim."[20]

He went on to state:

> "Now, I do not deny to any person the right to make any plan he chooses—whether it be a plan to fly to the moon or a plan to create a superior human being. But I do deny the planner the right to force me, or any other person, to conform to his plan ... Now you may ask: Did our great religious teachers practice social engineering? Was Jesus a social engineer? Recalling that I have defined social engineers as those who would re-make mankind in the mass by using the force of government, my answer is an emphatic no. For Jesus always appealed only to individuals. He asked that each one make a voluntary choice to follow God's way. He said to the individual, "The Kingdom of God is within you. That is, it does not lie in the group, or in the mob, or in the vote of the majority, but in the individual himself. Nor did Jesus ever appeal, or even suggest an

---

[20] http://www.americanthinker.com/2009/12/engineers_scientific_and_socia.html.

appeal, to the force of government for the accomplishment
of good works."

Like the Admiral, the founding fathers understood that that the
aim of social engineering is wholly incompatible with the highest
degree of personal freedom and liberty. They wisely recognized that
ignoring nature's laws in favor of man's laws was a recipe for tyranny
and destruction of free society.

> "What has always made the state a hell on earth has
> been precisely that man has tried to make it his heaven."
>
> *—F.A. Hayek*

The Proper Role of Government

As has been discussed, the principles of American government are based firmly on Locke's *law of nature,* which is the sum of dictates of reason required to secure peace and restrain men from invading the natural rights of others and doing hurt to one another. In Locke's *Second Treatise on Government* he wrote,

> "Political power then I take to be a right of making laws, for the regulating and preserving of property, and of employing the force of the community, in the execution of such laws, and in the defense of the commonwealth from foreign injury, and all this only for the public good."[21]

Based on this principle, the Founders conferred important yet limited duties on the federal government that were summarized by James Madison in *The Federalist No. 41* as follows[11]:

- Provide security against foreign danger.

- Regulate the intercourse with foreign nations.

- Maintain harmony and proper intercourse among the states.

- Restrain states from certain injurious acts.

Beyond these powers of the federal government, state governments assumed other limited powers that were necessary for securing peace and supporting commerce; these included establishing local defense and court systems as well as local infrastructure to support economic development and fund education. These limited duties conferred upon the federal and state governments amounted to what Thomas Jefferson described in a *1799* letter to Elbridge Gerry as "a government rigorously frugal and simple."[22]

---

[21] Locke, *supra.*

[22] Jefferson, *supra.*

Without advanced macroeconomic data at their disposal or explicit knowledge of what modern economists call **"Optimum Government Theory"**, the founding fathers established a system of government that not only protected the natural rights of the individual but provided the circumstances necessary for robust economic growth and prosperity. As a result, America grew to be the most productive economy in the world and her citizens came to enjoy the highest standard of living. However, this productivity and standard of living is being threatened today, along with the individual freedom we have come to take for granted, by an ever-expanding government that respects no Constitutional limits on its authority.

Optimum Government Theory

Optimum Government theory explains how **the size and scope of government have important effects on economic growth and prosperity.** In a study prepared for the Joint Economic Committee, Professors Richard Vedder and Lowell Gallaway explained Optimum Government theory as follows:

> "The output-enhancing features of government dominate when government is very small, and expansions in governmental size are associated with expansions in output. At some point, however, further expansion of government no longer leads to output expansion, as the growth-enhancing features of government diminish. Further expansion of government contributes to economic stagnation and decline."[23]

The most basic function of government, as expressed by Locke and the founders, is the protection of people and property. This is the **necessary foundation for the efficient operation of a market economy.** Therefore, the governmental provision of a certain limited

---

[23] Vedder RK, Gallaway LE. Government Size and Economic Growth. Prepared for the Joint Economic Committee. http://www.house.gov/jec/growth/govtsize/.pdf.

set of goods and services such as roads as well as national and local defense enhances economic growth. However, as governments move beyond these core functions, they adversely affect economic growth due to multiple mechanisms that include

- The disincentive effects of higher taxes

- The crowding-out effect of public investment in relation to private investment

- Diminishing returns as government undertakes activities for which they are ill-suited

- The government's interference in the economic growth process, because governments are not as good as markets in adjusting to changing circumstances and finding innovative new ways of increasing the value of resources."[24]

- Rent seeking as private businesses realize they can increase their market share by diverting public resources rather than improving productivity.

The bottom line is that **beyond an optimum level necessary for protecting people and property, government spending undermines economic growth by displacing private-sector activity.** Unlike the private sector which rewards individuals for hard work, personal character, productivity and ingenuity the public sector is mired in inefficiency and bogged down in the corruption of the political process.

---

[24] Chobanov. D., Mladenova, A. What Is The Optimum Size of Government. Institute for Market Economics. http://ime.bg/uploads/335309_OptimalSizeOf Government.pdf.

The following figure[25] depicts this optimum government theory nicely and is referred to as the Armey Curve after professional economist and Republican politician Dick Armey.

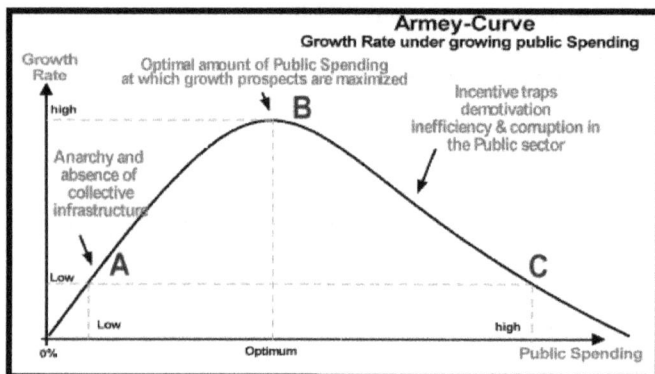

Armey-Curve
Growth Rate under growing public Spending

Figure 1. The Armey Curve.

The figure indicates that when government is very small (as a percentage of GDP) anarchy and the absence of collective infrastructure contribute to societal destabilization and low growth. Likewise, at high levels of government spending, incentive traps, demotivation, inefficiency and corruption in the public sector cause stagnation. The question then becomes, **what is the growth-maximizing level of government size?** Many economists have performed theoretical and empirical research to answer this question and we think it is important to understand their most influential findings.

Economic Data on the Optimal Size of Government

In an authoritative study prepared for the Joint Economic Committee of the United States Congress, Professors Richard Vedder and Lowell Gallaway examined the relationship between the five year economic growth rate and government spending in the United States.

---

[25] http://workforall.net/assets/Armey2.gif.

The authors found with 99% certainty that, over the time period 1796 to 1996, the size of the federal government that optimized economic growth was 11.06% of gross domestic product (GDP). They also found that over the time period 1957 to 1993, with 99% certainty, the size of state and local government that optimized economic growth was 11.42% of GDP (data for state and local spending could not be reliably analyzed prior to 1957). According to these results, economic growth was optimized when total government spending (federal + state and local) is equal to 22.48% of GDP).14 According to Vedder and Gallaway, "$80 billion in federal spending [beyond the optimum level] has associated with it an output-reducing impact of about $ 34 billion."

In another study prepared for the Joint Economic Committee, Professors Gwartney, Lawson and Holcombe performed an empirical analysis of data from 23 OECD countries and found a strong negative relationship between both (a) the size of government and the GDP growth and (b) increases in government expenditures and GDP growth. The following figure from Gwartney et al. clearly demonstrates an inverse relationship between the year-to-year growth of GDP and the size of government as a percent of GDP in the countries studied.[26]

According to Gwartney et al., "there is overwhelming evidence that both the size of government and its expansion have exerted a negative impact on economic growth during the last several decades. As government outlays in the United States have grown from 28.4 percent of GDP in 1960 to 34.6 percent in 1996, investment as a share of

---

[26] Gwartney J, Lawson R, Holcombe R. The Size and Functions of Government and Economic Growth. Prepared for the Joint Economic Committee. http://www.redaruba.com/hessels/nl/docs/The%20size %20and%20functions%20of%20government.pdf

GDP, labor productivity, and real GDP growth have fallen."[27] They further observe, "If government expenditures as a share of GDP in the United States had remained at their 1960 level, real GDP in 1996 would have been $9.16 trillion instead of $7.64 trillion, and the average income for a family of four would have been $23,440 higher."[28]

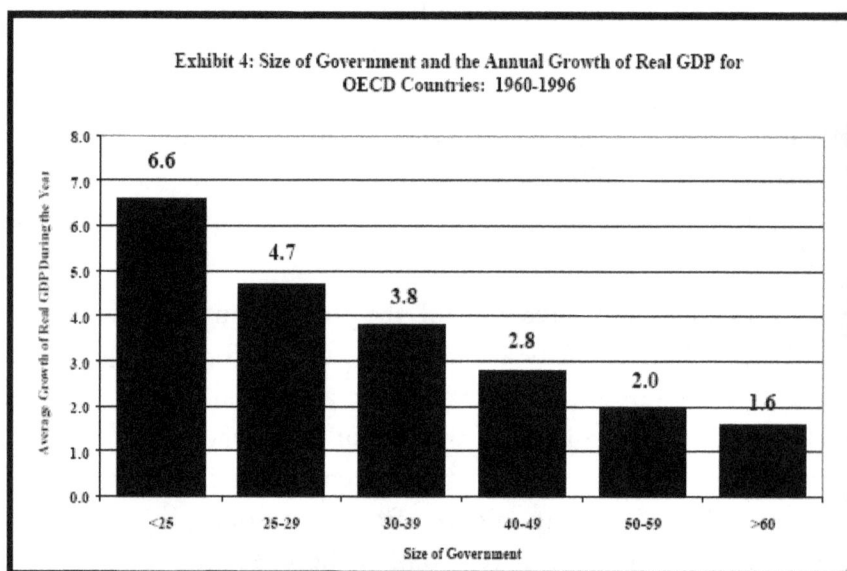

Figure 2. Size of government v. real GDP growth for 23 OECD countries.

In a recently completed paper, economists at the Institute for Market Economics (in Sofia, Bulgaria), have provided new estimates of the optimum size of government, using standard models, with data from 28 OECD member countries over the period 1970-2007. The authors reaffirmed the conclusions of earlier studies and concluded with 99% certainty that the optimal size of government to maximize economic growth is less than 25% of GDP.[29]

---

[27] *Ibid.*

[28] *Ibid.*

[29] Chobanov, *supra.*

"It has been well said that, while we used to suffer from social evils, we now suffer from the remedies for them. The difference is that, while in former times the social evils were gradually disappearing with the growth of wealth, the remedies we have introduced are beginning to threaten the continuance of that growth of wealth on which all future improvement depends."

F.A. Hayek

OUR CHALLENGE TODAY

Over the last 100 years the U.S. government has moved away from the proper understanding of its Constitutional foundation. Today we find ourselves in a position where the government's solutions which have been implemented over the course of many years to solve problems in society, as the result of overly broad interpretations of Constitutional authority, have left us with much bigger problems than the ones originally intended to be solved.

The following figure depicts total U.S. government spending from 1950 to the present.[30]

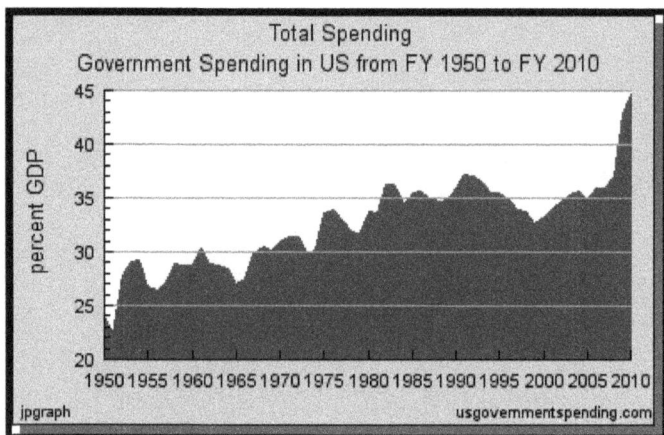

Figure 3. Government spending in US from FY 1950 to FY 2010.

Consider that our nation's unfunded liabilities, which most notably include Social Security, Medicare and Medicaid, are growing much faster than the rate of economic growth.[31]

---

[30] www.usgovernmentspending.com.

[31] http://www.gao.gov/cghome/townhall092905/img17.html

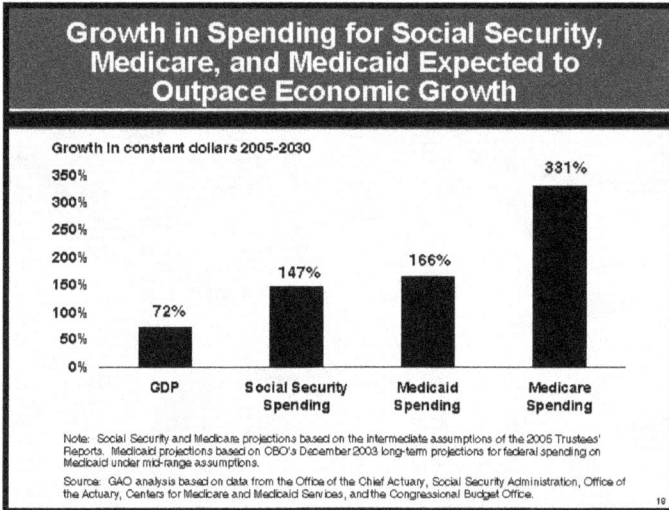

Growth in Spending for Social Security, Medicare, and Medicaid Expected to Outpace Economic Growth

Growth in constant dollars 2005-2030

- GDP: 72%
- Social Security Spending: 147%
- Medicaid Spending: 166%
- Medicare Spending: 331%

Note: Social Security and Medicare projections based on the intermediate assumptions of the 2005 Trustees' Reports. Medicaid projections based on CBO's December 2003 long-term projections for federal spending on Medicaid under mid-range assumptions.

Source: GAO analysis based on data from the Office of the Chief Actuary, Social Security Administration, Office of the Actuary, Centers for Medicare and Medicaid Services, and the Congressional Budget Office.

Figure 4. Growth in Social Security, Medicare, and Medicaid.

These programs were intended to alleviate a degree of suffering that would occur for program beneficiaries in the absence of such a safety net. However, these programs now threaten to bankrupt the country and pose a severe burden to taxpayers. More importantly they have encouraged many citizens to expect paternalistic support from the government and this attitude has become so pervasive that any talk of cutting benefits is met with a degree of incredulousness that all but stifles any hope for achieving meaningful progress in the area of debt reduction. If these programs aren't reformed in a meaningful way the country will soon be insolvent.

The problem of health care costs and inflation that we face today is a direct result of previous government policies aimed at addressing the problem of health care costs. Unfortunately, the problem is much worse now than when the government intervened in the 1960's and 70's.

In a policy review[32] prepared for the Commonwealth Foundation, Laffer, Arduin, and Winegarden describe how the government's involvement in the health insurance market has resulted in

> "[A] large and growing health care wedge—an economic separation of effort from reward, of consumers (patients) from producers (health care providers), caused by government policies ... The wedge is a primary driver in rising health care costs, i.e., inflation in medical costs."

The government's involvement in health care has become so complex that a 2,000-page bill that included an untold number of backroom deals with unions, special interests and industry lobbyists was proposed to achieve comprehensive reform that has ultimately resulted in higher premium rates for average Americans.

In a way similar to other prominent domestic issues such as social security and health care, **the recent housing crisis and recession is a lesson in unintended consequences.** In the government's attempt to solve the housing problem, it juiced the housing market and in conjunction with the Federal Reserve's lending policy, created an enormous housing bubble. In 1993 President Clinton significantly broadened the Community Reinvestment Act, originally signed in 1977, that mandated all FDIC insured banks to give more loans to lower income households (or less credit worthy borrowers). This move received broad political support. As a result of these changes, home ownership and inflation soared.

Furthermore, the government-chartered enterprises Fannie Mae and Freddie Mac enthusiastically purchased high-risk mortgages from lenders on the secondary mortgage market. Encouraged by the knowledge that high-risk mortgages would be swallowed up by

---

[32] *The Prognosis for National Health Insurance.* Prepared for the Commonwealth Foundation. http://www.commonwealthfoundation.org/docLi /20090831_LafferFull.pdf.

Fannie and Freddie, lenders had incentive to extend as many mortgages as possible regardless of the creditworthiness of borrowers.

Finally, in 2006 the Fed raised interest rates from 1% to 5.25% to avoid high inflation and suddenly adjustable-rate mortgage payments shot up, the demand for housing dried up, foreclosures multiplied, the credit crunch ensued, and heavily leveraged firms collapsed. The resulting financial crisis, caused by government intervention, has only led to more frenzied and hysterical government intervention, which shows no signs of letting up.

In the meantime, the clarity of President Obama and the Democrat's agenda has been revealed. Since taking office, Obama has rejuvenated his party's historical commitment to expanding government power, increasing taxes and unlimited spending.

The following figure[33] depicts the explosion of spending that has occurred under President Obama and the Democrats and reveals the painful truth that with total government spending approaching 45% of GDP our country is headed down the road to economic stagnation.

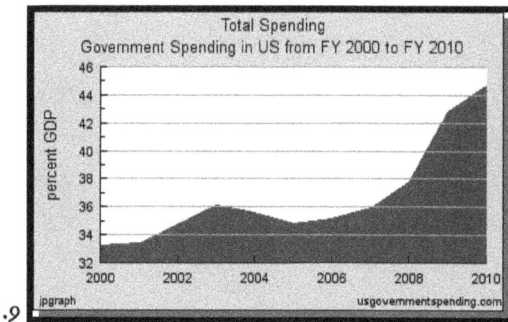

Figure 5. Government spending as a percentage of GDP.

---

[33] www.usgovernmentspending.com.

Thomas Jefferson must be either laughing or crying. After all, he favored "a government rigorously frugal and simple."[34] He favored the kind of government that was established by the U.S. Constitution; the kind of government that was intended to protect individual freedom and to secure peace. Over the last 100 years the government has morphed into an unrestrained monster that swallows up individual freedom, encourages irresponsibility, restricts economic growth and creates terrible problems wherever it turns.

In response to these problems, we should encourage a return to a natural law interpretation of the Constitution and discourage further government intervention to stimulate the economy, fix health care, prevent the oceans from rising, etc. and should instead advocate for legislation that decreases government involvement and respects the foundational American principles of individual freedom, personal responsibility and limited government. For without these principles society drifts, aimlessly, in a Sargasso Sea of competing claims, and politics is no longer subject to right but to force.

---

[34] Jefferson, *supra*.

Action Plan for Restoring America's Founding Principles

Step 1. Vote out the lifetime politicians. If the government won't create and enforce systematic term limits throughout the republican system, then it is our duty as citizens to enforce them. A lifetime politician is the biggest threat to individual liberty. Lifetime politicians, no matter how well intentioned, have irresistible incentives to pursue future political support in exchange for pursuing unwarranted exercises of government power that constrain our liberty and waste tax dollars. Whether Democrat or Republican, the lifetime politician has to go!

> "Whenever a man has cast a longing eye on office, a rottenness begins in his conduct."
>
> —*Thomas Jefferson*

> "And remember, where you have a concentration of power in a few hands, all too frequently men with the mentality of gangsters get control. History has proven that. All power corrupts; absolute power corrupts absolutely."
>
> —*Lord Acton*

Step 2. Fight all further government intervention to solve the current financial crisis. **The government cannot create jobs and it has no magic bullets for fixing the economy!** All it can do is move money from one sector of the economy to another, most of the time this money is being moved to reward political supporters. Corruption and social engineering are the end results! All the government does when it intervenes in the market is prop up some businesses at the expense of taxpayers and other businesses, creating massive uncertainty.

Step 3. Replace the current tax code, which is highly punitive and punishes productivity, with a **simpler and fairer tax code** that combines a flat tax with across the board consumption taxes. This way, productivity is rewarded. This would amount to a permanent tax deduction for many in the private sector, stimulating economic growth and job creation. It would also respect the foundational principles of American government most importantly the principle of equality under the law

Perhaps, no subject lends itself to a greater degree of demagoguery than the subject of taxation. This led Madison to write, in *The Federalist No.* 10, "The apportionment of taxes on the various descriptions of property, is an act which seems to require the most exact impartiality; yet, there is perhaps no legislative act in which greater opportunity and temptation are given to a predominant party, to trample on the rules of justice."

A review of our current tax code proves that justice has already been trampled on.[35]

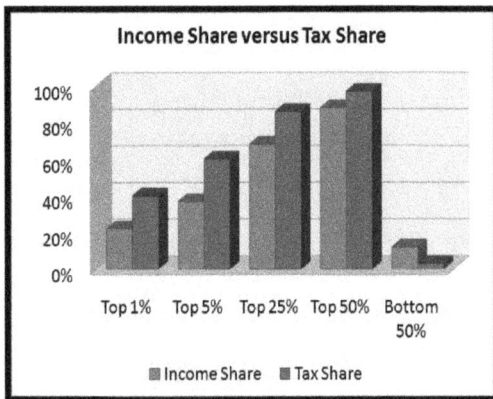

Figure 6. Income share versus tax share.

We must seek a return to justice in our tax code and advocate for a flat tax. We must restore the principle of equality under the law by taxing all citizens at the same rate.

---

[35] www.irs.gov/pub/irs-soi/08sprbul.pdf.

Step 4. We must aggressively reduce government spending. This will require that we make some very difficult decisions as **benefits will have to be cut.** This is absolutely necessary for putting America back on a path to permanent economic growth.

Our country is on the road to insolvency. The total debt that the Federal government has taken out in our names now amounts to $12.1 trillion or $87K per worker and the interest owed each year on the debt by every working man and woman alone amounts to $1820. What happens if we can't find buyers for this new debt?

In December of 2009 the world debt markets were rocked because Greece's credit rating was cut. The turmoil was caused because lower ratings mean higher probability of default on Greece's debt, threatening inflation, government bankruptcy and worse. The downgrade occurred because Greece has a government budget deficit of 13% of GDP and total debt that amounts to 113% of total economic production for one year. The United State's budget deficit for fiscal year 2009 (which ended in Sept) is 10% of GDP and total debt will amount to greater than 100% of GDP very soon.

If we cannot find purchasers of our debt, the economic, political and fundamental consequences will shake the foundation of our country with a ferocity worse than the great depression; a shift from which our nation might not recover.

Step 5. Never compromise the principles this country was built on! Today we hear incessant calls from our politicians to "come together", "compromise" and "cooperate in a bi-partisan way." But often these calls are baseless because on many fundamental policy issues there is no room for compromise. Many political "compromises" in the past have only led to an incremental expansion in the size and scope of government, a decrease in individual freedom and a decreased emphasis on personal responsibility.

Instead of compromise, patriotic Americans must fight to restore those principles of **Individual Freedom, Personal Responsibility** and **Limited Government** this country was founded upon. Stand up proudly and defend freedom from its enemies foreign and within. The liberty, happiness and prosperity of future generations depends on you.

> "At this auspicious period, the United States came into existence as a nation, and if their citizens should not be completely free and happy, the fault will be entirely their own."
>
> —*George Washington,* 1783

CONCLUSION. MY GRANDFATHER—AN AMERICAN LIFE

It will be easy to criticize this short book on grounds that it identifies some pretty general, widely recognized problems such as the massive expansion of government, exploding debt levels, and unfunded entitlement liabilities but offers no specific solutions to address them. In addition, it leaves a whole bunch of hot button social and military issues out. Criticism on those grounds would be valid however, it is not my intention to cure (as if anybody actually has one) all the country's problems but rather, to encourage individuals to organize around some very general and what I consider to be foundational principles of the American Republic. People who hold strongly to principles are more consistent in their ideas and actions. They can advocate their own positions with clarity and have more confidence to confront those who oppose them and the institutions and values they hold dear.

In my own life, nobody has embodied the American principles of liberty, personal responsibility, individualism, and self-reliance more than my Grandfather. He's not a hero in any commercial sense but his life and actions have been more influential on me than any sports legend or pop culture star. Francis DiMichelle was the son of first-generation Italian immigrants. He had many siblings and grew up relatively poor, especially by today's standards although I'm sure some of the stories have been indulged. He started working at a young age and that is probably where he began to learn the value of a dollar. He completed high school where I understand he was a good student but not exceptional and went on to learn the trade of electrician. He served in the National Guard where he furthered his electrical skills and eventually got hired by DuPont where he stayed for the remainder of his career.

From my Grandfather's humble beginnings he was able to provide an excellent quality of life for his children and grandchildren, no doubt a major driving force in his life. When I think about my Grandfather's life as a provider and patriarch I can't help but think of John Adams, one of our most influential founders and early American statesman. In a letter to his wife Abigail he wrote the following,

> "I must study politics and war, that our sons may have liberty to study mathematics and philosophy. Our sons ought to study mathematics and philosophy, geography, natural history and naval architecture, navigation, commerce and agriculture in order to give their children a right to study painting, poetry, music, architecture, statuary, tapestry and porcelain."

In this letter, I believe Adams provides the first glimpse of what became known as the American Dream - to come to this country, work hard and provide a better quality of life for your children and grandchildren than you had. My Grandfather did this and he did it well. He and my Grandmother passed up luxuries for themselves so their children and grandchildren could have more. Everything he earned, he earned it honestly and he wouldn't have accepted it any other way. But to only acknowledge my Grandfather's capabilities as a provider would do him a grave disservice and it would also dishonor America's founding principles.

In my Grandfather's role as provider he was the model for personal responsibility but in his constant pursuit of excellence throughout his life he personified the spirit of freedom and individualism. He is the embodiment of the early American Renaissance Man. This run-of-the-mill high school graduate excelled in many different things throughout his life. During his time at DuPont, he rose from an electrician to an engineer, who eventually would oversee the construction and design of corporate buildings. On the side, he built private homes as a hobby and after he retired, was hired to oversee the renovation of an historic building in the city of Wilmington. While I was aware that he did these things growing up I never appreciated it as much as I should have until a random occurrence where I was introduced to a man who worked with my Grandfather at DuPont. The gentleman was about my Grandfather's age, had a college degree in engineering and ran his own successful small business for heating and air conditioning installation. When he found out who my Grandfather was he could not conceal his admiration. He went on to tell me how my Grandfather could do it all and whenever any of the engineers ran into a problem they would call Franny.

I had no doubt this gentleman was genuinely telling the truth and at the time I wondered how my grandfather learned so much especially given the fact that he did not have the same level of formal education as the gentleman recounting the story. I pondered whether he could be a genius. I suspected not because that sort of thing is often passed down in the blood and I could find no evidence of genius in the family but what he did have was a voracious appetite for learning - a critical component for anyone interested in pursuing excellence and shaping his own life.

That learning is a lifelong process, and the most important learning is what you teach yourself, are the greatest lessons my Grandfather taught me. Sure, such slogans can be heard everywhere but how many people actually live them? The American Founders did (Franklin, Adams, Jefferson, etc...). Abraham Lincoln was almost entirely a self-taught man. To find evidence of their zeal for learning just read their personal writings and diaries. They tried to learn everything they could in order to become well-rounded and the best they could be. If they knew my Grandfather they would be impressed and probably would have a lot to talk about. I can imagine Jefferson and him talking for hours on end about the design and architecture of Monticello and the various home building projects my Grandfather undertook with much humbler resources at his disposal. But unlike

Jefferson, my Grandfather could perform much of the raw building in addition to the design.

During my life I have seen my Grandfather design and construct his basement as well as the basement in my parent's home. My Grandmother packed him a brown bag lunch most days, which he would eat in the middle of his eight-hour work day. You might ask, "Why was he working eight hour days to finish our basement while fully retired?" Because that's just how he is and I presume he was anxious to see the finished product. I also saw him complete a magnificent landscaping project in the back of his home, which consumed most his back yard and was capable of being showcased in *Home and Garden Magazine*. Then there was the beautiful book case he built for me before going away to medical school, which I mainly wanted so I could start a collection and become well read like him. I'm catching up.

There's probably more I could say about my Grandfather but I think this paints a reasonably good picture of the man. I'm quite sure if more people were like him this country would be in a better place and our moral compass as a nation would still be intact. I'll freely admit that he's not the most stylish in his tube socks, khaki shorts, and loafers, his wide-rim glasses are fifty years out of date, he cannot use a computer or cell phone, and he occasionally says things that aren't the most polished but no one embodies the American principles of individual freedom, personal responsibility, self-reliance and individualism more than my Grandfather. He never lamented over his own circumstances growing up or asked what anybody could do for him, especially not the government; he only asked to be left alone so he could set out down new paths, armed with nothing but his own vision, a strong desire to pursue his ambitions, and plenty of stuff to read to help him get there, and of course, my Grandmother without whom none of it would have been possible. That's an American life we should all strive for.

ABOUT THE AUTHOR

Andrew was born and raised in Wilmington, Delaware and attended Salesianum high school. He graduated with honors in Biochemistry and Molecular Biology from Ursinus College. He went on to attend Jefferson Medical College in Philadelphia where he received the JeffHOPE© Student Award for devotion to the underserved population of Philadelphia. After graduating medical school he joined the Army Reserves Medical Core.

He is currently a medical resident at Jefferson University Hospital in Philadelphia and next summer will begin a cardiology fellowship at Penn State Hershey Medical Center in Hershey, Pennsylvania.